Wildflowers
of Northern California

T0166290

Adventure Quick Guides

YOUR WAY TO EASILY IDENTIFY WILDFLOWERS

Adventure Quick Guides

This Adventure Quick Guide features 168 of the most common and showy wildflowers you'll see north of a line connecting San Luis Obispo and Death Valley. Whether you're exploring northern California's coastal dunes and estuaries, the majestic redwood forests, or hiking through its foothills, inland valleys, or amid the parks and peaks of the Sierra Nevada and Cascade mountains, this guide has you covered.

With its great variety of climate and habitats, northern California has more plant diversity than anywhere else in the country. The central and northern coasts each support more than 1,400 species of wildflowers, shrubs, trees, and grasses. Each of the two northern mountain ranges are home to 1,700-plus plant species. This guide introduces you to the most common northern California wildflowers found alongside roadsides, trails, in meadows and valleys, as well as those found in the plateaus or deserts.

GEORGE MILLER

Longtime botanist and nature photographer George Miller has explored the West for 30 years and has been published in books, magazines, and newspapers. He's written six guidebooks to plants and animals of the Southwest, including *Landscaping with Native Plants of Southern California* and *Wildflowers of Southern California*, as well as five smartphone wildflower guides. He is a member of the Native Plant Society of California.

Cover and book design by Lora Westberg
Edited by Brett Ortler

Cover image: Western Columbine by George Miller

All images copyrighted.

Bill Bouton: Butterfly Mariposa, Golden Fairy Lantern, Hairy Star Tulip, Mountain Lady Slipper, Yellow Mariposa Lily **By Calibas (Own work) [Public domain], via Wikimedia Commons:** Blue Dicks/Wild Hyacinth **Allison Carson:** Mission Bells **Dena Grossenbacher:** Sierra Onion **Jerry Kirkhart:** Indian Warrior **Jonathan Norberg:** leaf icons **By PiPi (Own work) [Public domain], via Wikimedia Commons:** Creeping Wild Ginger **Ben Salzberg:** California Pitcher Plant (main) **Shutterstock:** Fivespot **By Stickpen (Own work) [Public domain], via Wikimedia Commons:** California Golden Violet, Firecracker Flower, Golden Eardrops, Purple Chinese Houses **Miguel Vieira:** Red Larkspur

10 9 8 7 6 5 4 3

Wildflowers of Northern California
Copyright © 2018 by George Miller
Published by Adventure Publications
An imprint of AdventureKEEN
310 Garfield Street South
Cambridge, Minnesota 55008
(800) 678-7006

www.adventurepublications.net
All rights reserved
Printed in China
ISBN 978-1-59193-753-1

KEY

- Wildflowers are sorted into four groups by color and organized within groups from smaller to larger blooms.
- Leaf attachment icons are shown next to each wildflower.
- Descriptions include important facts such as cluster shape, number of petals, or center color to help you quickly identify the species. Size information is sometimes included as well.

LEAF ATTACHMENT

Wildflower leaves attach to stems in different ways. The leaf icons next to the flowers show alternate, opposite, whorled, perfoliate, clasping, and basal attachments. Some wildflower plants have two or more types of leaf attachments.

 ALTERNATE leaves attach in an alternating pattern.

 OPPOSITE leaves attach directly opposite each other.

 BASAL leaves originate at the base of the plant and are usually grouped in pairs or in a rosette.

 PERFOLIATE leaves are stalkless and have a leaf base that completely surrounds the main stem.

 CLASPING leaves have no stalk, and the base partly surrounds the main stem.

 WHORLED leaves have three or more leaves that attach around the stem at the same point.

 CLUSTERED leaves originate from the same point on the stem.

 SPINES are leaves that take the form of sharp spines.

PARTS OF A FLOWER

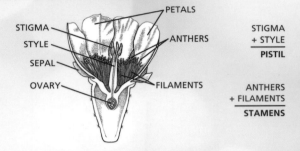

CLIMATE, GEOGRAPHY, AND PLANT DIVERSITY

With the highest mountain in the contiguous United States (Mt. Whitney, 14,505 feet), and the lowest point (Death Valley, minus 282 feet), northern California is one of the most biodiverse regions on the planet. The combination of cold Pacific currents and towering mountain ranges that run north-south creates five major climate zones. Starting along the coast, three variations of the unusual Mediterranean climate are present, each with its own distinct pattern. One features cool summers followed by cool winters; another has coastal fog in the summer, and yet another boasts hot summers and cool winters. Many of the plants that adapted to these conditions grow nowhere else in the world.

The warm, semi-arid, steppe climate of the interior valleys, now almost totally irrigated for agriculture, receives enough rain for wildflowers and grasses but not trees. The jagged mountain spine that bisects California traps the moist, life-giving ocean winds on the western slopes, while the rain-starved eastern slopes are the driest deserts in North America. In the summer, Death Valley sizzles at 115 degrees, while a few dozen miles away conifer forests thrive at 10,000 feet. A myriad of micro-climates exist in each region, and they are often determined by such variables as elevation, slope, and the direction to which they are exposed. Northern California's active geology also influences the vegetation. Tectonic effects have created serpentine soils, which lack calcium, in the region; calcium is necessary for plant growth. Over the eons, many plants have adapted to these infertile soils and grow nowhere else. In other areas, plant communities have adapted to a variety of other soils.

All of these varying habitats make northern California one of the best places on the planet to find wildflowers.

Abronia latifolia

Yellow Sand-Verbena

Prostrate stems on beaches; spherical clusters of trumpet-shaped flowers; thick oval leaves

Berberis aquifolium

Oregon Grape

Evergreen shrub; clusters of 30–60 small, yellow flowers; leaflets lined with prickles; blue berries

Eriogonum umbellatum

Sulfur Flower Buckwheat

Stems leafless, up to 12 inches tall; spherical clusters of yellow flowers; leaves oval, mat-forming

Foeniculum vulgare

Sweet Fennel

Clumps to 6 feet tall; tiny flowers in flat-topped clusters; leaves hair-like; roadside weed

Pterospora andromedea

no leaves

Woodland Pinedrops

Erect, reddish, leafless stems; spike of tiny, urn-shaped flowers; parasitic on conifer roots

Solidago velutina

Three-nerve Goldenrod

Stems to 5 feet tall with slender clusters of tiny flowers; leaves taper to base and tip

Senecio triangularis

Arrowleaf Groundsel

Stems to 5 feet tall; flower heads have 8 rays, yellow disk; leaves narrowly triangular, toothed

Ericameria nauseosa

Rabbitbrush

Thick bush to 6 feet; dense clusters of tiny, tubular flowers; leaves narrow, gray/green

Yellow to Orange

Agoseris aurantiaca

Orange False Dandelion

Dandelion-size orange flowers grow on leafless stalks from a basal rosette of leaves; milky sap

Dasiphora fruticosa

Shrubby Cinquefoil

Shrubby to 3 feet tall; 5 oval petals, showy stamens; leaflets narrow, pointed, crowded

Corallorhiza maculata

no leaves

Spotted Coralroot Orchid

Stems leafless, red or yellow, pencil-thin; red spots on flower lower lip; occurs in forests

Corallorhiza striata

no leaves

Striped Coralroot Orchid

Red or yellow, leafless, stems to 18 inches; spike of flowers, yellowish with red-purple stripes

Ehrendorferia chrysantha

Golden Eardrops

Stems to 5 feet tall; 2 curving outer petals, 2 erect central petals; leaves have fern-like lobes

Erysimum capitatum

Wallflower

Stems to 2 feet; spherical flower clusters, 4 petals, yellow or red-orange; pods parallel stems

Holocarpha virgata

Yellowflower Tarweed

Branching stems to 4 feet, sticky; flowers have yellow notched rays, purplish anthers; tiny leaves

Hypochaeris radicata

Hairy Cat's Ear

Stem to 30 inches; many notched ray florets, reddish on backside; leaves lobed, hairy; roadside weed

Lupinus arboreus

Yellow Bush Lupine

Shrubby to 6 feet; spikes of yellow flowers; fruit pod hairy; leaf with 5–20 radiating leaflets

Mimulus bicolor

Yellow & White Monkeyflower

Stems to 10 inches; upper flower lip white, lower lip yellow with red spots; narrow leaves

Mimulus guttatus

Yellow Monkeyflower

Stems 2–3 feet; lower flower lobe bearded with red spots; leaves rounded; in wet areas

Potentilla anserina

Silverweed Cinquefoil

Stems prostrate, red, spreading; 5-petaled flowers; leaves have narrow leaflets along midrib

Potentilla gracilis

Slender Cinquefoil

Stems 8–30 inches tall; 5-petaled flowers; leaves have 5–7 radiating, toothed leaflets

Ranunculus californicus

California Buttercup

Stems 1–2 feet tall; flowers with 9–17 petals, many stamens; leaves with 3 oval, hairy, pointed lobes

Verbascum blattaria

Moth Mullein

Stems to 3 feet; yellow or white flowers with purple centers; leaves toothed; roadside weed

Verbascum thapsus

Mullein

Stems to 6 feet tall; spike of small yellow flowers; large, fuzzy basal leaves; roadside weed

Yellow to Orange

Sedum spathulifolium

Broadleaf Stonecrop
Succulent; stems to 8 inches; clusters of up to 30 flowers; basal leaves rounded, tapering to stem

Dudleya farinosa

Powdery Dudleya
Rosette of succulent, often red-tipped leaves; flower stalk 4–14 inches with small red leaves

Calochortus amabilis

Golden Fairy Lantern
Stems to 20 inches; nodding flowers; 3 spreading sepals, 3 fringed petals; leaves grass-like

Agoseris grandiflora

Giant Dandelion
Stems to 2 feet; 150+ rays tipped with tiny teeth; striped backside; leaves lobed

Heterotheca sessiliflora

False Golden-Aster
Mat-forming or with stems to 2 feet tall; 8–18 rays and yellow disk; lance-shaped, hairy leaves

Diplacus aurantiacus

Sticky Monkeyflower
Bush that is 3–4-feet high/wide; yellow-orange to red trumpet-shaped flowers; lance-shaped leaves

Erythronium grandiflorum

Avalanche Lily
Leafless stems; nodding yellow flowers with petals curled backwards; lance-shaped leaves

Fritillaria affinis

Checker Lily, Mission Bells
Up to 48 inches tall; nodding flowers; yellow-green to brown-purple, mottled petals; lance-shaped leaves

Madia elegans

Common Madia

Stems to 3 feet tall; 5–22 yellow rays often with a maroon base, yellow disk; narrow, hairy leaves

Viola pedunculata

California Golden Violet

Plant 2–15 inches; lower petal with dark lines; heart-shaped leaves with teeth

Arnica mollis

Rough-leaf Arnica

Stems to 12 inches tall; 2-4 pairs of hairy, lance-shaped leaves; colonizes mountain meadows

Bidens laevis

Bur Marigold

Wetland plant to 2 feet; 7–8 rays, orange-yellow disk; lance-shaped linear leaves; edges serrated

Calochortus luteus

Yellow Mariposa Lily

Up to 18 inches tall; yellow petals with reddish marks; hairs on median; linear leaves fade by summer

Eriophyllum lanatum

Woolly Sunflower

Stems to 2 feet; flowerhead with 5–13 yellow rays; yellow disk; leaves lobed along midvein

Grindelia hirsutula

Gumweed

Stems to 5 feet, erect to prostrate; 10–60 rays; yellow disk, resinous buds; oblong leaves

Layia platyglossa

Coastal Tidytips

Stems to 2 feet; flowers with 5–18, two-tone (rarely solid) rays with 3 notches; yellow disk

Oenothera elata

Evening Primrose
Leafy, branching stems to 8 feet; funnel-shaped flowers; 4 petals; leaves get smaller upward

Eschscholzia californica

California Poppy
Flowers blanket hillsides with 4 gold-to-orange petals; leaves with fern-like lobes; yellow sap

Hymenoxys hoopesii

Orange Sneezeweed
Up to 3 feet; 14–26 yellow-orange ray flowers; large yellow disk; clasping, lance-shaped leaves

Mentzelia laevicaulis

Giant Blazing Star
Stem to 3 feet; showy flowers, 5 tapering petals, many stamens; sandpapery, wavy, and lobed leaves

Opuntia polyacantha

Plains Prickly Pear
Clumps one pad high; dense spines; solid yellow or magenta flowers; fruit is a spiny, tan capsule

Wyethia mollis

Mountain Mule Ears
Stems to 2 feet; flower has 6–15 rays; hairy, broadly lance-shaped leaves are up to 16 inches long

Balsamorhiza sagittata

Arrowleaf Balsamroot
Stems to 16 inches, one flower-head each; basal leaves triangular, up to 4 inches wide and 12 inches long

Fremontodendron californicum

Flannelbush
Shrub to 15 feet; yellow petals rounded with tiny tips; leaves leathery with 3 rounded lobes

Western Snakeroot

Shrubby to 28 inches tall; clusters of pink to white tubular flowers; triangular to oval, toothed leaves

Sea Thrift

Leafless stem; 6–18 inches; dense ¾-inch diameter cluster of tiny flowers; grasslike leaves; coastal

Showy Milkweed

Up to 4 feet tall; clusters of rose-pink flowers; seed pods covered with warty prickles; milky sap

Pygmy Bitterroot

Ground-hugging stems; petals pink with darker stripes; long, narrow leaves; high meadows

Spreading Phlox

Mat-forming; pink, white, or pale blue flowers; narrow, pointed leaves; open forests

Mountain Heather

Stems to 16 inches; flowers pink to purplish with long stamens; needle-like, crowded leaves

King's Crown

Stems to 20 inches tall; flowers in flattish clusters; crowded, pointed, succulent leaves

Meadowsweet

Shrub to 3 feet tall, wide; round clusters of rosy-pink flowers; oval-elliptic, toothed leaves

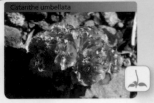

Pussy Paws

Red prostrate, radiating stems; spherical clusters, red or white flowers; red or yellow stamens

Twinberry

Shrub to 6 feet; reddish to yellow paired tubular flowers; fruit 2 black berries with red bracts

Pink Honeysuckle

Sprawling vine; pink tubular flowers; hairy, curled petals; red fruit; oval leaves with hairy edges

Firecracker Flower

Leafless stems 1–3 feet; cluster of tubular, nodding flowers with green tips; grass-like leaves

California Fuchsia

Shrubby; funnel-shaped, red to orange flowers; protruding stamens; linear to oval leaves

Prairie Smoke

Red stalks to 8 inches tall; three nodding, urn-shaped flowers; feathery seed clusters

Cardinal Catchfly

Stems branching, 1–2-feet tall; tubular flowers with 5 deeply cut petals with pointed lobes

Snow Plant

Scarlet, leafless stems to 12 inches; found on forest floor with a spike of urn-shaped flowers

Zeltnera venusta

Charming Centaury

Branching stem to 20 inches tall; flowers have 5 pointed petals, white throat; narrow to oval leaves

Chamerion angustifolium

Fireweed

Stems leafy, chest-high; spikes of pink flowers, 4 petals; forms dense stands on mountain slopes

Castilleja arachnoidea

Cobwebby Paintbrush

Stem 12 inches; bracts red to dull yellow, hairy; flowers greenish, beak-shaped; linear, lobed leaves

Castilleja chromosa

Desert Paintbrush

Stem 18 inches; bracts red-tipped, lobed; yellowish, beak-shaped flowers; linear, lobed leaves

Castilleja linariifolia

Wyoming Paintbrush

Stem to 3 feet; red, lobed bracts; greenish, beak-shaped flowers; linear leaves, rolled inward

Castilleja miniata

Scarlet Paintbrush

Stem to 30 inches; bracts red-tipped, lobed; yellow beak-shaped flowers; lance-shaped leaves

Delphinium nudicaule

Red Larkspur

Stem to 20 inches tall lined with flowers; petals point forward, spur backwards; fan-shaped leaves

Dicentra formosa

Bleeding Heart

Stems to 18 inches; dangling, heart-shaped flowers; rose-purple petals; fern-like lobed leaves

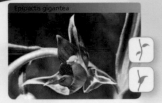
Epipactis gigantea

Giant Helleborine Orchid

Leafy stems to 3 feet; veined pink to orange flowers; lower petal wiggles in breeze; pointed leaves

Ipomopsis aggregata

Skyrocket

Stems to 3 feet; red, trumpet-like flowers; spreading petals with white spots; threadlike leaves

Pedicularis densiflora

Indian Warrior

Stems to 20 inches tall with dense spike of showy tubular flowers and bracts; fern-like leaves

Keckiella corymbosa

Red Beardtongue

Up to 3 feet tall; topped with a cluster of tubular flowers; 3 lower and 2 upper lobes; oval leaves

Penstemon newberryi

Mountain Pride

Mat-forming; stems to 12 inches lined with tubular flowers; throat hairy; leaves oval, toothed

Penstemon rostriflorus

Bridge Penstemon

Stem to 40 inches lined with hairy tubular flowers, lower lip bent back; linear, toothless leaves

Primula jeffreyi

Sierra Shooting Star

Stem to 2 feet; petals swept upward with a white to yellow band above a maroon base

Rosa californica

California Rose

Thicket-forming shrub with prickles; flowers have 5 reddish-pink petals and showy yellow stamens

Salmonberry

Leafy shrub; pinkish-red flowers; yellow to red, edible berries; leaves have 3 toothed leaflets

Western Columbine

Up to 2 feet tall; nodding flowers have yellowish-tipped petals and long, straight, red spurs

Cobweb Thistle

Stem up to 9 feet; webby, spiny oval with filament-like red, pink, or lavender flowers; spiny leaves

Scarlet Monkeyflower

Stems 1–3 feet; flowers with red to orange upper and lower lips; oblong leaves; found in wet soils

Lewis Monkeyflower

Stems 1–3 feet; flowers pink to rose, spreading upper and lower lips; oblong leaves; mountains

Farewell to Spring

Stems to 3 feet; cup-shaped flowers; 4 pink to purple petals, usually with a red patch; linear leaves

California Pitcher Plant

Mottled basal leaves; pitcher-shaped; flower stem 2–3 feet; 5 reddish-green petals; darker veins

California Leopard Lily

Stem to 6 feet; petals curl back; red-orange with maroon spots, tips often red; moist soils

White to Green

Actaea rubra

Baneberry
Clumps to 3 feet; rounded clusters of tiny flowers; toothed leaflets; red or white fruit; **toxic**

Bistorta bistortoides

Western Bistort
Up to 24 inches tall; dense oblong spike of tiny white to pinkish flowers; lance-shaped leaves

Anaphalis margaritacea

Pearly Everlasting
Up to 3 feet tall; pearly white flowers, some with yellow florets in the center; narrow leaves

Anemopsis californica

Yerba Mansa
Up to 1 foot tall; spike with 4–9 white, petal-like bracts below cone with smaller white bracts

Achillea millefolium

Common Yarrow
Stems 1–3 feet tall; flat clusters of tiny white flowers; fernlike aromatic leaves

Angelica hendersonii

Henderson's Angelica
Up to 5 feet tall; umbrella-like clusters with 20–45 spheres of flowers; lance-shaped leaflets

Angelica tomentosa

Woolly Angelica
Up to 2–6 feet tall; umbrella-like clusters with spheres of small flowers; lance-shaped, toothed leaflets

Daucus carota

Queen Anne's Lace
Up to 4 feet tall; umbrella-like cluster, with a tiny maroon flower in the center; parsley-like leaves; roadside weed

White to Green

Antennaria corymbosa

Flat-top Pussytoes

Mats 2–6 inches tall; clusters of tiny, white, thread-like flowers; spoon-shaped, woolly leaves

Apocynum androsaemifolium

Spreading Dogbane

Erect, branching to 3 feet tall; bell-shaped, slightly nodding flowers; broad, pointed leaves

Aruncus dioicus

Bride's feathers

Bushy to 7 feet tall; plume-like clusters of tiny creamy flowers; leaflets serrated with long points

Asclepias fascicularis

Narrow-leaf Milkweed

Stems to 3 feet; round clusters of small, creamy-pink flowers; narrow leaves; milky sap

Eriogonum nudum

Naked Buckwheat

Stems leafless; up to 16 inches; round clusters of white to pink flowers; elliptic leaves, woolly below

Eriogonum wrightii

Wright's Buckwheat

Mat-forming; flower clusters bloom along stem, white with a red mid-stripe; woolly leaves

Gaultheria shallon

Salal

Coastal thicket-forming shrub; up to 6 feet; white to pink flowers; black fruit; oval, leathery leaves

Lepidium virginicum

Peppergrass

Stems to 2 feet tall; dense clusters of small flowers, 4 petals; seeds are disks on the short stems

White to Green

Heliotropium curassavicum

Heliotrope

Stem 4–24 inches; small bell-shaped flowers; throat yellow turning purple; oval, fleshy leaves

Maianthemum racemosum

False Lily of the Valley

Stem 12–36 inches; plume of tiny feathery flowers; sword-like leaves with distinct parallel veins

Maianthemum stellatum

Star Solomon's Seal

Stems 12–28 inches; clusters have one star-shaped flower per tiny branch; sword-like leaves

Marah oregana

Coastal Manroot

Vine; bell-shaped cream to white flowers; hairy, lobed leaves; roundish, prickly fruit

Orthilia secunda

Sidebells Wintergreen

Stem to 8 inches; green to cream, bell-shaped flowers found on one side of stem; elliptic leaves

Phacelia heterophylla

Varileaf Phacelia

Stems to 4 feet tall; flower cluster is dense, curved, hairy; lower leaves lobed, upper unlobed

Sambucus nigra

Blue Elderberry

Shrub/small tree; flat-topped flower clusters; blue-black fruit; leaves with 3–9 leaflets along midrib

Xerophyllum tenax

Beargrass

Flower stem to 6 feet tall; tipped with dense flower cluster; grass-like leaves grow in a thick basal clump

White to Green

Western Spring Beauty

Stem to 6 inches; 5 white to pink petals, often lined or with yellow base; lance-shaped leaves

Western Virgin's Bower

Vine; flowers with 4-5 hairy petals, showy stamens; leaves have 5–15 leaflets; fruit a silky plume

Mountain Lady's Slipper

Stem up to 2 feet; upper petals and sepals brown; pouch-like lip white; elliptic leaves

Granite Prickly Phlox

Woody stems to 16 inches; funnel-shaped, petals white to pale pink; crowded, prickly leaves

Wild Strawberry

Small white flowers and red berries; basal leaves with 3 leaflets with coarse teeth

Wild Licorice

Leafy stems; up to 1–4 feet; seed pods covered with hooked prickles; leaves have 13–19 leaflets

Rattlesnake Plantain Orchid

Stem 3–15 inches lined with 10–48 small, white-greenish flowers; elliptic, white-streaked leaves

Tall White Bog Orchid

Stem to 4 feet; fragrant flowers; side petals spreading, lip drooping; folded, lance-shaped leaves

White to Green

Cow Parsnip
Up to 8 feet tall; umbrella-shaped clusters of small, white flowers; leaves with 3 broad, pointed lobes

Fremont's Death Camas
Stem to 2 feet tall; star-like flowers; 6 petals with green basal dots; slender, arching leaves

Corn Lily
Small flowers on branching stalks; tall corn-like stems in moist areas; broad, strongly veined leaves

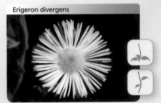

Spreading Fleabane
Branching stems to 16 inches; white to lavender-tinted rays; yellow disk; buds nod; narrow leaves

Philadelphia Fleabane
Leafy, hairy stems to 30 inches; flowerheads with 150+ rays; clasping upper leaves

California Pipevine
Woody vine; pipe-shaped greenish-brown dangling flowers with purple stripes; heart-shaped leaves

Marsh Marigold
Stems to 1 foot; white petals, purple buds, many stamens; heart-shaped, fleshy leaves; found in wet areas

Monument Plant
Stalks 2–6 feet; whorls of purple-spotted green flowers; basal rosette of broad leaves

White to Green

Leucanthemum vulgare

Ox-eye Daisy
Clump-forming; 2-foot stems; leaves lobed or with blunt teeth; invasive to roadsides, meadows

Rubus parviflorus

Thimbleberry
Leafy, thornless shrub 3–6 feet tall; red, edible berries; maple-like leaves with 5 pointed lobes

Argemone munita

Prickly Poppy
Stem and leaves prickly; flowers with large, delicate petals and showy yellow stamens

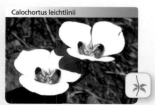
Calochortus leichtlinii

Leichtlin's Mariposa Lily
Up to 2 feet; petals have yellow, hairy base, dark spot; basal leaves linear, wither by flowering

Calochortus tolmiei

Hairy Star Tulip
Up to 4–16 inches; 3 densely hairy petals white, pink, or purple with spotted base; linear leaves

Calochortus venustus

Butterfly Mariposa
Up to 2 feet; 3 petals with variable colors in white, pink, purple, red, or orange; dark central spots

Nemophila maculata

Fivespot
Sprawling stems; 5 white petals with dark veins, tipped with blue; oval leaves, 5–9 lobes

Datura wrightii

Sacred Datura
Robust, sprawling plant, 5 feet across; trumpet-shaped flowers; oval leaves to 10 inches long

Mertensia ciliata

Streamside Bluebells

Stems 3–4 feet; fragrant, tubular hanging flowers; elliptic, blue-green leaves; wet meadows

Monardella villosa

Coyote Mint

Up to 2 feet tall; rounded cluster of pink to lavender thread-like petals; oval, fragrant leaves

Pedicularis groenlandica

Elephant Head

Stems to 30 inches; flowers resemble a tiny elephant head; fernlike leaves; wet meadows

Prunella vulgaris

Self-heal

Short spikes of small hooded flowers with a fringed lower lobe; elliptical leaves; forms colonies

Viola adunca

Hooked-spur Violet

Blue to violet flowers on 4-inch stem; whitish throats have dark lines; oval to triangular leaves

Allium campanulatum

Sierra Onion

Umbrella-like clusters of 10+ star-like flowers; purple to rose petals; flat, grass-like leaves

Astragalus lentiginosus

Freckled Milkvetch

Clumps to 3 feet wide; reddish stems; tubular, purple and white flowers; inflated fruit pod

Collinsia heterophylla

Purple Chinese Houses

Stems to 2 feet tall; whorls of snapdragon-like flowers, lower petals purple, upper petals white

Delphinium depauperatum

Dichelostemma capitatum

Slim Larkspur

Stem to 15 inches; 3–15 flowers with spreading petals and spur; round, deeply lobed leaves

Blue Dicks/Wild Hyacinth

Rounded clusters of tubular flowers with 6 bluish-purple to pink petals; grass-like leaves

Gilia capitata

Lupinus albifrons

Bluehead Gilia

Dense, rounded clusters of flowers have 5 petals and extended stamens; fern-like leaves

Silver Bush Lupine

Shrubby to 16 feet tall; spikes of violet to lavender flowers; 6–10 hairy, radiating leaflets

Lupinus latifolius

Sisyrinchium bellum

Bigleaf Lupine

Stems 1–6 feet tall; spikes of blue to purple or white flowers; 5–11 radiating leaflets

Western Blue-eyed Grass

Dense clumps of flat, grass-like leaves; flower has a yellow throat and 6 petals with pointed tips

Solanum elaeagnifolium

Solanum xanti

Silverleaf Nightshade

Stems and leaves prickly, covered with silvery hairs; star-shaped flowers; fruit is a yellow berry

Chaparral Nightshade

Shrubby, 3 feet tall; petals blue disk with a green base; fruit a greenish berry; dark green leaves

Cichorium intybus

Chicory
Stems to 6 feet; petals light blue with 5 tiny points, anthers darker; common roadside weed

Asyneuma prenanthoides

Nodding Harebell
Stems to 30 inches; blue, dangling flowers, 5 petals curved back, long protruding stamen

Brodiaea californica

California Brodiaea
Branching stems to 18 inches; flowers funnel-shaped, 6 bluish-to-violet spreading petals

Calypso bulbosa

Fairy Slipper Orchid
Stem to 8 inches; magenta to pink spreading sepals and red-spotted lip; one oval leaf

Castilleja exserta

Purple Owl's Clover
Stems hairy; spikes of lobed, rose-purple bracts surround yellow- to white-tipped flowers

Cirsium arvense

Canada Thistle
Noxious weed up to 4 feet; flower-head with purple spines; tassel-like flowers; leaves lobed, spiny

Dieteria canescens

Purple Aster
Stem to 2 feet; flowerheads with 8–25 blue to purple rays; yellow disk; narrow leaves

Linum lewisii

Blue Flax
Pointed buds, 5 petals; narrow, pointed leaves hug the stem; delicate flowers last one day

Erigeron glacialis

Erigeron glaucus

Wandering Fleabane
Up to 18 inches; blue, purple, or pink rays; yellow disk; lance-shaped leaves smaller up the stem

Seaside Fleabane
Clump-forming; up to 12 inches tall; 80–300 purple, pink, or white rays; large, yellow disk; coastal

Nemophila menziesii

Penstemon davidsonii

Baby Blue Eyes
Stems to 12 inches; blue flowers with a white center; leaves with 5–13 lobes along midrib

Davidson's Penstemon
Mat-forming; tubular, blue to lavender flowers; white-woolly inside; oval leaves; found in the mountains

Penstemon rydbergii

Aconitum columbianum

Rydberg's Penstemon
Stems 8–24 inches; tubular blue to purple flowers with gold hairs found in whorls; moist meadows

Columbian Monkshood
Stems 1–6 feet; flowers with hood-like upper petals; leaves deeply lobed; all parts **toxic**

Asarum caudatum

Iris douglasiana

Creeping Wild Ginger
Flowers have 3 long-tapering, hairy, maroon petals; heart-shaped leaves; found as forest groundcover

Douglas Iris
Stems 6–18 inches; flowers purple to cream with purple veins, gold base; leaves flat, slender

Adventure Quick Guides

Only Northern California Wildflowers

Organized by color for quick and easy identification

Simple and convenient—narrow your choices by color and leaf attachment, and view just a few wildflowers at a time

- Pocket-size format—easier than laminated foldouts

- Professional photos of flowers in bloom

- Similar colors grouped together to ensure that you quickly find what you're looking for

- Leaf icons for comparison and identification

- Easy-to-use information for even casual observers

- Expert author is a skilled botanist and photographer

Get these *Adventure Quick Guides* for your area

NATURE/WILDFLOWERS/CALIFORNIA

ISBN 978-1-59193-753-1 $9.95

5 0 9 9 5

9 781591 937531

PUBLICATIONS
Adventure
an imprint of AdventureKEEN